HICKIE

AN AMERICAN HERO

Hickie

Growing up in Indiana in the 1940's and 50's during my young years, I hunted, fished, and trapped many of the rivers, creeks, and woods in the area. I was inspired to write this exciting book about the many wonderful memories with my dad, **HICKIE**, **an American Hero**, and holder of the prestigious **Carnegie Medal for Bravery,** and an avid Sportsman,

Bill A. Hicks, Author

HICKIE

An American Hero

iUniverse, Inc.
New York   Bloomington

HICKIE
AN AMERICAN HERO

iUniverse books may be ordered through booksellers or by contacting:

iUniverse
1663 Liberty Drive
Bloomington, IN 47403
www.iuniverse.com
1-800-Authors (1-800-288-4677)

Because of the dynamic nature of the Internet, any Web addresses or
links contained in this book may have changed since publication and may
no longer be valid. The views expressed in this work are solely those of
the author and do not necessarily reflect the views of the publisher, and
the publisher hereby disclaims any responsibility for them.

ISBN: 978-1-4502-1543-5 (sc)
ISBN: 978-1-4502-1544-2 (ebook)

Printed in the United States of America

iUniverse rev. date: 04/19/2010

I may not have anything in the eyes of the world or by the world's standards, but this one thing I do have: Good childhood memories. The world didn't give them to me and the world can't take them away. — Bill Hicks

INTRODUCTION

This book is to give honor to my Dad, who was my Hero and a true American Hero, when I was growing up in the 1940's and '50's in Cambridge City, Indiana, my Small-town, U. S. A. Although he was not blessed with many material things, my dad always wanted the best for me and was always there when I needed him. He was a man full of God-given knowledge of the outdoors and nature, knowledge also enhanced by his dad and passed on to me as I was growing up. Where my dad went, there I was also. I was his sidekick. So, to my fishing teacher, coon-hunting partner, mushroom-hunting confidant, squirrel-hunting buddy, rabbit-hunting chum, and my first baseball coach, this is written for you.

On August 22, 1990, my Dad's last words to me were, *"Goodbye, son. Dad's not going to make it this time. The Lord be with you."* And then he went to be with the Lord.

I also want to acknowledge with gratitude the many school teachers, coaches, and community leaders in Cambridge City, Indiana for their dedication and patience with me as I was growing up. They inspired character and were living models that steered me in the right direction as I watched how they conducted their lives.

Each made a unique mark on my life. Their rare commitment to my peers and me has paid off in our generation, and consequently in generations to come. They were true mentors, and by their example I and many others have obtained some of what a wise person once wrote in the Proverbs: *"Happy is the man that finds Wisdom, and the man that gets understanding, for the merchandise of it is better than silver, and its gain finer than gold. She is more precious than rubies: and all the things a man can desire are not to be compared to her. Length of days is in her right hand; and in her left hand riches and honor. Her ways are pleasant, and all her paths are peace. She is a tree of life to he who gains her, and happy is every one that retains her."*

"This book is also written to men everywhere who grew up in SMALL TOWNS in the U.S.A. One of the greatest gifts we were given as kids was a vast supply of natural resources like the small creeks, ponds, lakes and woods that hemmed in our rural towns and communities. Without fear or care we were blessed to have the freedom to play, roam, and take advantage of God's limitless creation. Nature was our backyard. In this day of peer pressure, video games, cell phones, high speed internet, availability of drugs and other temptations, it is my intention to challenge, to inspire, and encourage young people today who are growing up in small towns all over America, to get outdoors and take advantage of all the natural resources you have around you. `

"LOCAL HEROS MAY NEVER HAVE BEEN AS IMPORTANT AS THEY ARE TODAY, AN ERA WHERE THERE ARE SO FEW NATIONAL HEROES. TODAY THE NATIONAL HUNGER FOR HEROES MAY BE BEST SATISFIED ON A SMALL SCALE, WHERE A SINGLE MAN, WOMAN, OR CHILD MAY EXEMPIFY THE SELFLESS BRAVERY AMERICA HAS LONG HONORED."

—*Wall Street Journal*

"I do not expect to stimulate or create heroism by this fund, knowing well that heroic action is impulsive; but I do believe that,
if the hero is injured in his bold attempt to serve or save his fellows,
he and those dependent upon him should not suffer pecuniary."
--Andrew Carnegie

HICKIE

AN AMERICAN HERO
CORNEGIE HERO FUND COMMISSION
AWARDED TO EDWARD HICKS

Dublin, Indiana, August 19, 1938, Edward Hicks, 25, laborer, attempted to save Auburn A. Money, 37, and Clarence Zook, 32, laborers, from burning, When crude oil vapor exploded in the vicinity of a storage tank from which sludge was being removed, flames extended 160 feet from the tank, which then exploded. Hicks, who was just inside the fire area, ran from the flames and extinguished fire on his clothing. Money, and Zook, who were near in the tank, called for help. Shielding his face with one arm, Hicks ran into the flames about 25 feet, reached Money, and Zook and aided them to a point beyond the flames. Zook died that night, Money died from burns later the next day. Hicks was seriously burned and was disabled for more than 19 weeks.

The headline in Richmond, Indiana's local newspaper, - *The Palladium Item*, read, *"Carnegie medal awarded to Dublin man for rescue work in fatal tank blaze."*

(Richmond is Wayne County's county seat just a few miles east of Cambridge City.)

"Gee, that's swell" was the first comment of Jesse Edward Hicks, a 25-year-old Dublin resident, when notified Friday night by the Palladium-Item that he had been awarded a bronze medal by the Carnegie Hero Fund commission in Pittsburgh, Pennsylvania. Hicks will get the medal in recognition of his heroism in rescuing his fellow workers fatally burned in an explosion of a crude oil storage tank at Dublin on August 19.

The recipient of the award, who is five feet, three and on-half inches tall and weighs 169 pounds is the son of Mr. and Mrs. John

Hicks and resides with his parents and three brothers on Main Street in Dublin.

Hicks was confined to the Henry County Hospital in New Castle for three months and eighteen days after the explosion, finally recovering from severe burns about the back, arms and head.

'Hickie,' which he prefers to be called, was working near Auburn A. Money, 37, and Clarence Zook, 32, when crude oil vapor exploded near a storage tank from which sludge was being removed. Flames leaped 160 feet when the tank also exploded. The crude oil almost filled the reservoir, which surrounds each of the tanks at the field of the Gulf Refining Company and burned for several days.

The resume of the case as reported by the Carnegie commission in an Associated Press dispatch continued:

Hicks, who was just inside the fire area, ran from the flames and extinguished fire from his clothing. Money and Zook, who were near the tank, called for help. Shielding his face with one arm, Hickie ran into the flames, reached Money and Zook, and aided them to a point beyond the flames. Zook died that night, leaving behind his wife, and three small children. Money died the next day. Hicks was severely burned and disabled for many months.

Hicks told the Palladium-Item that the AP dispatch was the first word he had received of his award. He also said he had been offered a job by the Crude Oil Contracting Company of Tulsa, Oklahoma, in whose employ he was working at the time but that he had turned it down, declaring the memory of 'that h___ at the field west of Dublin' prevented his accepting.

The Carnegie Hero bronze medal is inscribed with these words: 'Greater love hath no man than this, that a man lay down his life for his friends.'

CARNEGIE HERO FUND COMMISSION

The two-fold mission of the Carnegie Hero Fund Commission: To recognize persons who perform acts of heroism in civilian life in the United States and Canada, and to provide financial assistance for those disabled and the dependants of those killed helping others.

We live in a heroic age, Andrew Carnegie wrote in the opening lines of the Commission's founding Deed of Trust in 1904. *Seldom are we thrilled by deeds of heroism where men or women are injured or lose their lives in attempting to preserve or rescue their fellows.*

Carnegie's "hero fund," administered by a 21-member commission in Pittsburgh, was charged with honoring whom he called the "heroes of civilization," whose lifesaving actions put them in stark contrast to the "heroes of barbarism, (who) maimed or killed" their fellow man. That the mission of the Hero Fund as set forth by Carnegie is unchanged over 105 years, despite massive upheaval in the social and world order, is testament both to his foresight and to essentially unchanging human nature. Approved by the founder, the Commission's working definition of a hero as well as its requirements for awarding remain largely those that were for an award must be a civilian who voluntarily risks his or her life to an extraordinary degree while saving or attempting to save the life of another person. The rescuer must have no full measure of responsibility for the safety of the victim. There must be conclusive evidence to support the act's occurrence, and the act must be called to the attention of the Commission within two years.

Those who are selected for recognition by the Commission are awarded the Carnegie Medal, and they, or their survivors, become eligible for financial considerations, including one-time grants, scholarship aid, death benefits, and continuing assistance. To date, more than 8700 medals have been awarded, the recipients selected from more than 80,000 nominees.

Carnegie Medal Is Awarded to Dublin Man for His Rescue Work in Fatal Tank Blaze

SECOND MAN DIES AFTER BLAST, FIRE AT HUGE OIL TANK

Clarence Zook, Dublin; Auburn Money, Straughn, Succumb at New Castle

HICKS IS "SATISFACTORY"

Blaze Is Second at Dublin Field During August; Cause of Blast Not Known

DUBLIN, Ind. Aug. 19—Auburn Money, 25-year-old Straughn resident, died at 5:00 p. m. today in the Henry County hospital at New Castle, the second victim of a fire that followed the explosion of an 38,000-barrel crude oil tank near here early this morning. Cause of the blast has not been determined.

Clarence Zook, 32 years old, of Dublin, married and the father of three small children, died at the hospital about 9 o'clock this morning from burns received from the blast at the Gulf Refining company's field, one mile southwest of here.

Ed Hicks, about 25 years old, of Dublin, was removed to the office of a Cambridge City physician for treatment of burns, but later was taken to the Henry County hospital. Attaches of the hospital late last night reported his condition as "satisfactory."

Betty Jackson, Robert Kinneman, Mary Boyer and Clara Johnson, all of Dublin, were singed by the flames and were treated at Cambridge City. Kinneman and the three women had brought Hicks to the field, where he went on duty at midnight. Hicks, assisting Zook and Money in cleaning the 38,000-barrel crude oil tank, was working at the base of the tank. Then the blast occurred, blowing the steel roof to the south side, and into the reservoir which surrounds each tank. Flames enveloped Zook and Money. Hicks was burned as he aided Zook and Money from the blazing sludge.

The exact cause of the explosion could not be determined. One theory was that it was caused by ignition of gasses accumulating from the residue in the tanks, which were practically empty of oil. It was advanced that the blast might have been set off from sparks from the automobile's exhaust.

Homes Shaken

Homes in the immediate locality were shaken. The oil burned itself out about 9:30 o'clock this morning.

Today's explosion and fire is the second that has occurred at the field since its erection in 1920, and only two weeks after lightning struck one of the tanks. About 200,000 gallons of oil burned in the fire which lasted 48 hours. Shortly after this first fire, a train bearing several tanks of sludge oil was derailed near Knightstown, causing oil in one of the tanks to catch fire and burn.

Funeral services for Zook will be held Saturday afternoon at 4 o'clock in his Dublin home, with burial following at Riverside cemetery. Friends may call at the Wiseman Funeral home in Cambridge City until 2 a. m. Saturday, and after that time at the residence.

Zook is survived by the widow, Retha; three small children; his mother, Mrs. Ida Zook Krahl of Dublin; five sisters, Mrs. Myra Morris of Dublin, Mrs. Hazel Zook of Hollywood, Fla., Mrs. Ethel Martin of New Castle, and Mrs. Emma Rocksback of New Castle, and three brothers, Ralph and Carl of Richmond, and Glen, residing in Michigan.

Last rites for Money have not been completed. They will be announced later. He resided alone at Straughn, being divorced some time ago. His wife has remarried. A sister, Mrs. Andrew Rausch, Richmond, survives.

Hicks is a single man.

Edward Hicks

FIELD

(Continued from Page One)

A fire caused by lightning, a train bearing several tanks of processed sludge from the Dublin field was derailed near Knightstown, with sludge in one of the tanks catching fire. The derailment was said to have been caused by a broken journal.

Money is living alone at Straughn. He and his wife were divorced some time ago. He since has remarried.

Hicks is a single man.

An inspection of the ground adjoining the destroyed tank early this morning revealed Zook's car had seen little action. Citizens saw the upholstering still wet smouldering in the rear seat of the car. A man's scorched belt, torn in two pieces and the zipper from a sweater front also were seen.

Surviving of Mr. Zook are the widow, Retha; three small children; his mother, Mrs. Ida Zook Krahl of Dublin, five sister, Mrs. Myra Morris and Mrs. Ruth Stoke, Dublin; Mrs. Emma Rhodenbach, Mrs. Ethel Martin, New Castle; Hazel Zook of Florida, and three brothers.

Mr. Zook was born Feb. 27, 1906, at Winchester, and had been at Dublin 16 years.

Funeral services will be held at the home in Dublin Saturday at 4 p. m. Burial will be in Riverside cemetery. Friends may call at the Wiseman Funeral home, Cambridge City, until 2 a. m. Saturday and after that time at the late residence.

HICKS IMPROVES FROM BURNS OF OIL TANK BLAST

NEW CASTLE, Ind. Aug. 20.—Ed Hicks, 25 years old, of Dublin is recovering satisfactorily at the Henry County hospital in New Castle, attaches reported late last night, from burns received in a blast fatal to two men at the Gulf Refining company's crude oil station near Dublin Friday.

Clarence Zook, 32 years old, of Dublin died Friday from burns suffered in the oil explosion and Auburn Money, 25 years old, of Straughn died in the hospital Friday night.

Funeral services for Zook were held Saturday afternoon at his home in Dublin, and burial took place at Riverside cemetery.

Last rites for Money will be conducted Monday morning at 10:30 o'clock in the Howard Funeral home, Cambridge City. The body was removed at the funeral home in relatives to the Funeral home in will be taken home in Sunday. lawn or

Articles in local newspaper about the fire incident

CARNEGIE MEDAL

The Carnegie Medal is a bronze medallion three inches in diameter and is awarded to civilians who risk their lives to an extraordinary degree saving or attempting to save the lives of others.

Andrew Carnegie's profile in relief dominates the obverse of the medal. The reverse carries as background, in low relief, the outline of the United States and Canada, the Commission's field of operation, and the seals of the two countries appear in high relief. The reverse of the medal centers on the cartouche, or inscription plate, which carries an embossed statement naming the rescuer, the rescued, and the place and date of the heroic act. The cartouche is adorned with laurel, ivy, oak, and thistle, respectively signifying glory, friendship, strength, and persistence - the attributes of a hero. A verse from the New Testament encircles the outer edge: "Greater love hath no man than this, that a man lay down his life for his friends" (John 15:13)

CARNEGIE MEDAL

Front and back of the Carnegie Medal

This is what appears on the reverse side of the metal:

EDWARD HICKS
WHO ATTEMPTED TO SAVE
AUBURN A.MONEY and CLARENCE ZOOK
FROM BURNING
DUBLIN, IND.
AUGUST 19, 1938

Hickie and Clarence Zook were friends and hunting buddies for many years before Zook's death. Hickie and Zook's widow kept in contact after the incident. After a several months of courting they were married, and later the author of this story was born to them.

FAMILY

Hickie and Retha married and divorced each other twice by the time I was twelve years old. Those were not easy years for any of us in the family, but we all survived. I chose to stay with my Dad and we made our home with my grandparents, whom I loved very much.

My grandfather, John, was a railroad man for the Pennsylvania Railroad. The railroad had two sets of tracks and ran through Cambridge City. The tracks were vital to some businesses in our town. When the tracks were torn out it closed many working places in our area.

Granddad worked as a section hand for 46 years. When the railroad ties would get old or wear out the men on the section would have to replace them and then tamp the ties down. Sometimes they would have to replace sections of track with new rail. He used to say that the railroad was the hottest place to work in the summer and the coldest place to work in the winter.

We used to hunt asparagus and strawberries on the Pennsylvania Railroad every spring. The strawberries were small but very sweet. It took forever to pick a quart. The asparagus was plentiful on the railroad. We would hunt from South Green Street to the first bridge in Dublin.

About three quarters of the way up there was a spring of water by the railroad. We always had to stop and get a big drink of that clear cold water.

My dad worked for the railroad also. He and my grandfather worked for the same boss. One time the boss called my dad a bad name. Hickie was all but five foot three and one half inches, but he was scrappy, and never took any guff from any one. He was also a boxer. Dad turned around and hit him and the boss fell to the ground. When dad came home that evening he told my mom what had happened, and he was worried that he might have to go to jail. Later on that evening the police came to our house and took him down town. I remember I thought I would never see him again because I thought he would have to go to prison. It was a very scary time for the rest of us for several hours that night, but after the facts came out he was released and the police brought him back home. Needless to say, he lost his job.

My grandfather was a very hard-working man. I never knew anyone that worked any harder than he did. Every spring he would plow up two gardens. One was by the side of the house and the other was in the old canal bottom. In the garden by the side of the house he turned the soil with a hand shovel, which was no easy task.

Granddad would work all day on the railroad, and then come home, clean up for dinner, eat dinner, then work in the garden until dark. He loved every minute of it. It wasn't work to him.

The garden by the house was for personal use for Grandma and him. The canal garden was for the whole family, which we all worked. We grew sweet corn, tomatoes, potatoes, peas, green beans, cucumbers, pickles, onions, peppers, sweet potatoes, pumpkins, okra, and all kinds of vegetables. Grandpa loved pickles and onions. We all used to sit outdoors under one of the shade trees and shell peas and break green beans.

My grandmother used to can vegetables and we would have them all winter. She would make homemade ketchup that was really good on the fried potatoes in the wintertime. For the bottles she would use Nehi pop bottles. She had her own bottle capper. She would put the cap on the bottle and press the capper down on the bottle and that would seal it. There is nothing like homemade ketchup out of a Nehi pop bottle in the wintertime.

In the summer when Grandpa worked on the railroad, he would have Grandma fix an onion quartered and two slices of buttered bread and that would be his lunch. Many times he would take an onion and a fried egg sandwich
On Saturdays about noon Grandpa would get cleaned up and walk down the old canal path to town and get him a beer. That was it, he would take his time, chat with the people, and drink one beer and then walk back home on the old canal path. That was his thing to do.

Walking along the old canal path at night was kind of scary, as there were no streetlights and it was pitch dark. My uncles used to whistle when walking home at night on the path. I supposed they thought that would scare away any suspicious persons that might be lurking around. Sometimes there would be a dark shadow of a body coming from the opposite direction and you would get a little nervous, until you realized it was one of your neighbors and then you would take a sigh of relief.

Grandmother was a very energetic woman. She was busy all the time. She was a short, redheaded Irish lady and very high-spirited. You did not want to get on her bad side. She washed our clothes every Monday summer and winter. Our water came from outside, so every Monday I would help draw water and Grandma would heat it on the gas stove in a big wash tub and wash our clothes and hang them out on the clothesline to dry.

On Tuesdays she would always do her ironing. She ironed everything from blue jeans to underwear. I was the best-dressed kid in school. When we had holes in our socks, she would sit down and darn them. She had a small gourd she would put inside the sock where the hole was and sew the hole up. I didn't have fancy clothes, but she made sure I always had clean clothes.

After each day was over she would clean the dishes, and then sit down in her chair and read her bible. Many times she would fall asleep in her chair. Sometimes she would watch television. She and Grandpa would always watch Gunsmoke.

It was my grandmother that kept our family together. She started the Hicks reunion, and every year we would have sixty or seventy relatives come from towns in Indiana, Michigan, and Ohio. Like most reunions, you got to see relatives you don't normally see except once a year. She had a way about her, and her cooking for us was one of her ways of showing her love for us. She was a wonderful cook and baker, and she saw to it that we had three meals every day.

Sundays were always special. Grandma would always fix a feast for lunch and my uncles and their wives would come over to join in on the meal. We would have meals like chicken and dumplings, or fried chicken, or baked chicken and dressing, or dried dumplings with broth, or maybe we would have roast beef with noodles, which was one of Hickie's favorites. Desserts were her specialty. She would always have one cake and usually two pies. She would make most of her cakes from scratch. Our favorites were devils food and angel food. I used to enjoy watching her in the kitchen, and I made sure I stayed out of her way. She would mix all her cakes by hand because she never had the convenience of an electric mixer. It seemed like every time she would start to mix a cake she would light up a cigarette, sit down and whip away with her wooden spoon.

One time as she was whipping the cake batter, I saw the ashes on her cigarette fall into the mix, but she just kept on mixing. No one ever knew the difference.

We had our own apple tree in the back, so we had lots of apple pie. One of my uncles loved cherry pie so she would bake a cherry pie just for him. I loved her banana cream with meringue topping. My dad's favorite was her butterscotch with meringue topping.

Saturday's was Grandma's day to go to town. She would go by herself, but sometimes she would take me. Grandma would doll up, powder her face, and put her fancy hanky in her purse and made sure half of it was sticking out. She would walk down the path next to the old canal, and make her way down town, do her shopping, and then go to the movies. We had a theater called Angelo's and she would go and watch Roy Rogers, who was her favorite. Sometimes she would get so involved in the movie she would shout out, "Kill'em Roy! Kill them crooks!"

One fall windy day, Grandma went to town and while she was gone I got the idea I would help her out by raking and burning some leaves like the neighbors down the street were doing. I raked all the leaves into the ditch in front of the house and set them on fire. I didn't expect the wind to spread the flames toward the house, threatening to engulf it! Thankfully, I heard the fire alarm, and shortly here came the fire trucks. It was time for me to take cover, so I hid in the bushes and watched the action.

Here came Grandma right on cue while the firemen were putting out the fire. She asked, "What on earth happened here?" The fireman responded that someone had called in to report that a youngster had set some leaves on fire and when we got here there was no one in sight. After a worried search, Grandma finally found me in the bushes and coaxed me to come out. "Why did you hide?" she asked. "I was afraid I would be punished!" She put me in her arms and hugged me and said, "No one is going to punish you." Her suggestion to me was that when burning leaves the next time I should make sure it is with an adult. Kids sometimes think the worst scenario. I hid because I thought I would get a hard whipping and possibly put in jail to learn my lesson, when all it took was some tender, loving care.

Grandma smoked Chesterfield and Old Gold cigarettes. She kept them on the kitchen cupboard shelf out in the open. It seemed an open invitation to take one or two every now and then. I never got accused of taking them, but my uncle Dave, who also lived at Grandma's from time to time, always got the blame. Sometimes I would sneak a couple cigarettes from the shelf and my friend David and I would go over to the old canal and hide in the tall horseweeds and smoke a cigarette. We would light them with Grandma's kitchen matches, which I also sneaked.

One evening Hickie came home from work, looked at me and said, "You have been smoking cigarettes, haven't you?" I said, "Well….." and he said, "Don't lie to me." I didn't get a whipping but I got grounded. Hickie seemed to know the times when I smoked, and I never could figure it out how he knew.

Later on when I was older, I asked him how he knew. He said, "When you lit up those cigarettes with Grandma's kitchen matches, you would always singe your eyebrows, and that was a dead giveaway."

There were lots of things to do in the summer when I was growing up. When we were not at the ball diamond playing, it seemed like at least some time during every day my friend, David, and I would play pitch and catch in Grandma's front yard. Grandma had flowers everywhere and if you missed the ball on one end of the yard, it would go into Grandma's flowers and sometimes into the garden. On the other end if you missed the ball, it would go into Grandma's other flowers. Grandma would come out and say, "Now, you boy's keep that ball out of my flowers and out of my garden!" When we were older, David and I both played four years of high school baseball. Dave was a catcher and I played in the outfield.

Granddad and his Brother George

Grandmother Hicks

THE CANAL

The **Whitewater Canal**, which was built between 1836 and 1847, spanned a distance of seventy-six miles and stretched from Hagerstown, Indiana, to Lawerenceburg, Indiana, and on to the Ohio River.

There was the need for a high-speed transportation system back then that could link the Whitewater Valley to the Ohio River. Before the canal, farmers had to transport their goods and livestock to Cincinnati Ohio, on badly rutted and often impassable roads. The journey to Cincinnati could take several days.

Very little is left of the Whitewater Canal today. Some tow path was bought by the Whitewater Valley Railroad Company and has been used in various train operations over the years. A section of the rail line is still in use as a tourist railroad. The Whitewater Valley Railroad operates between Connersville and Metamora, Indiana. The remains of many of the canal locks on this section of the canal can still be seen as well as the diversion dam near Laurel, Indiana, that is still in service for the restored canal section in Metamora.

The most visible area of the Whitewater Canal that exists today is in Metamora. Here the Canal Era is recreated and tourists can stroll through a nineteenth century town. There are antiques, shopping, eateries, and you can even take a horse drawn ride on the canal.

The Whitewater Canal was a short venture, but it left an everlasting mark on the communities it traveled through. The canal extended north of Cambridge City, to Hagerstown. The canal came right in town in Cambridge City. At the end of it was an old cement lock. I can remember playing there often with my friends. We would choose up sides and play war and try to conquer the dam from one another. We made mud balls with a rock in the middle, and we would pull up horseweeds and make spears out of them. The horseweeds, after you would shake off the dirt, had a very pointed end that looked like a javelin. The battle would go on for hours. Finally somebody would get hurt, or we would just get tired of playing. We were lucky no one ever got his eye put out.

My friend, Bud, and I were coming home from grade school one icy winter day. We walked home on the frozen creek that went through town and down the street from where we lived. (We used to call the creek "Poop Creek." Back then we didn't have the sewage system we have today.) We were having so much fun sliding on the ice we forgot to get off on the street that took us home. We just kept going until we ended up in Mt. Auburn and that is where the ice broke. Bud fell in under the ice and into the water waist deep. He had such a helpless look on his face as he was sliding under the ice. I helped pull him out, but the damage was already done. He was soaking wet up to his waist. We decided we had better head for home due to the circumstances and I'm sure our parents were wondering why we weren't home yet. By the time we got home Bud's pants were frozen solid and it was all he could do to walk. When his mother met us at the door she was furious, and I got all the blame.

I think the reason I got blamed was because during the fall season we were playing war in the old canal and Bud and I were on different teams. The ammunition we used were spears made from horseweeds. We would throw them at each other and I hit Bud in the face much too close to his eye. I walked him home after the incident and his mom met us at the door and gasped at his bloody face. I told her what happened and she sent me home. I really felt bad about that accident because Bud was one of my best friends.

When I was younger, we lived at 236 West Maple Street, which was one block west of the old canal. On that street there were 13 or 14 boys and we were all about the same age. On the south side of Maple Street was an open lot. There were many scrub ball games played on that lot. In the game of scrub, we would normally have three or four batters. When one batter made an out he would have to go to the outfield and work his way back up then everyone else moved up one position. After pitcher you moved up to batter.

One time, I got this older kid out at first base. He got mad and shoved me down. I was a little smaller than him, but that didn't make any difference. I got up and shoved him back. We got into a real fistfight swinging and hitting each other. When his nose started to bleed the other kids pulled us apart. Oh, it was an awful sight, blood running out his nose and all over his shirt. I felt so bad, like Yeah.

That was the end of that. There comes a point sometimes in life when you have to stand up for yourself, that was one of those times. He never bothered me after that.

In the fall after school we played football on the lot. We hardly ever had any schoolwork to bring home, so we would play ball until suppertime. We played tackle and we had some knock down drag out games. We did have some bloody noses in some of those games, but that was a sign you were tough.

One time this high school kid who played on the football team came over to where four of us were playing. He said, "I'll take on all four of you." We told him okay. Before the game was over we tore his shirt completely off his back. His folks owned the local dairy, and they had a black top driveway on their property with a basketball goal. It was a treat to play basketball there as the rest of us all had gravel alleys to play in. We would go over to their house and play basketball, and while we were there his mother would sometimes treat us with ice cream cups that were made in their dairy. They were a little half-pint cardboard cups, red with white stars on them. She would give each of us a wooden spoon to eat it with also. Boy, what a treat.

Ms. Hothouse was the Juvenile Correctional Officer of Wayne County when I was growing up. When ever you did something wrong, they would always tell us that they were going to send us to Ms. Holthouse if we didn't behave. We kids formed this impression of her as being a big old woman with this big whip that she would use on you and throw you in jail. We didn't know it then, but I'm sure she was a very nice lady.

Before my grandparents owned the little five-room house on the north edge of Cambridge City and next to the canal, they lived in Dublin, Indiana, on US 40 on the north side of the road, two miles west of Cambridge City. They lived there several years. When I was five years old I decided to go visit my grandparents in Dublin. I walked over to U S 40 and headed west. I knew where I was going. I made it to Mount Auburn, when a city police car pulled along side of me and ask me where I was going. I told him I was going to my grandparents' house. He asked where they lived, and I told him they lived in Dublin. He asked me my name, and when I told him he knew where I lived. He said maybe I had better go with him. By the time we got to the house my mother was out frantically looking for me. Well, needless to say, after that incident Hickie devised a harness for me. When I played in the back yard, the harness would be snapped on a rope, and hooked to the clothesline. No more running away.

The canal had other sources of food for us other than the garden. It also provided meat for us in the fall and winter in the form of a vast supply of wild game. I used to walk up the canal squirrel hunting, and later on in the winter I would hunt rabbits. Occasionally I would jump up a covey of Hungarian Partridge and get one or two. Sometimes I would walk into a covey of quail when I wasn't expecting it and they would just scare the pants off of me.

Hickie would tell hunting and fishing stories to me about him and my Grandfather when he was a young man. One of the stories that he told was when my grandfather and his brother, George, used to hunt rabbits with an old Lafever double-barreled 12-guage shotgun. They only had one shotgun between them so they would flip a coin to see who would go first. Only when one would miss would the other one get to shoot. Sometimes one of them would go a whole day without getting a turn. Back then you could kill as many rabbits as you wanted in a day, and some days they killed as many as 20. They would take their kill home and clean them, keep what they needed for food, then sell the rest to those who could afford them and give the rest away to friends and neighbors.

As a boy when we would sell wild game, we always left the fur or hair on a hind leg. People would know then what they were buying. I use to go door to door and sell rabbits in the winter. In the summer I would sell squirrels that were completely skinned and cleaned. In the springtime when Dad and I hunted asparagus and brought it home, mom would bundle it up and I would sell it door to door.

I would take two of the dogs we owned rabbit hunting with me up the canal. One was a toy Collie, we named Patsy, and the other was a Springer Spaniel we named Lucky. They loved to go with me, and they loved to hunt. I would put one dog on one side of the canal and the other one on the other side and we would hunt up the canal. I killed a lot of rabbits by hunting that way.

Did you ever skin a rabbit? The way to skin a rabbit is first, you should have already pulled his head off in the field and let it bleed. We used to pull the head off, grab both ears and pull the head in half and let the dogs have it. Hickie said it would make the dogs hungrier for the next rabbit. When cleaning a rabbit you hold him by the hind legs with one hand and take the other hand and grab its fur on its belly. Hold firmly and pull the fur all the way off the underneath side. Next, you do the same thing on the back of him, pulling the fur down and not stopping until it is completely off. You should have one clean rabbit with no hair left on the carcass. You get better at it the more you clean.

I will never forget the first gun that was given to me. It was a present from my great cousin, Hershel. I was six years old at the time. It was a very small 22 caliber single shot bolt action rifle. I was so little I couldn't pull the hammer back. Later on when I was a little older I would take it with me when I ran my traps. It was handy, particularly after a night's snow. The next morning when running my traps I could see the tracks where a rabbit had laid up, I would follow the tracks till they led to the rabbit and then shoot it. The nice thing about that was no buckshot. It was a clean kill.

I was about nine or ten years old before I was allowed to use a shotgun. It was the old Lafever 12-gauge my grandpa and his brother used to use when they hunted rabbits. I remember the first time I was hunting with it. Dad and I were hunting rabbits on the Pennsylvania Railroad. A rabbit jumped up and ran out my way. I took aim on that rabbit and was so excited I squeezed both triggers and shot both barrels at the same time. Back then we couldn't afford very many shells. After I had pulled both barrels, and missed the rabbit, dad would only give me one shell at a time to shoot. I learned real soon to make sure of the first shot, and eventually I became a pretty good shot and was allowed to use two shells.

CENTRAL SCHOOL

Central school is located on U S 40 on the north side of Main Street. When I was in the first grade, the teacher had a Victor wind-up floor model record player. One day when we were standing in line, I was positioned just beside the record player's handle. Standing there I started turning the handle and it fell off. Well I thought I had broken it, so I tried to put it on top of the player without anyone seeing me but I got caught. I thought I was in big trouble. Here came the teacher but instead of being upset she smiled. She put it back on and then showed me that one way was to wind up the player and the other way was to take the handle off.

The second grade was in the basement. That year on Armistice Day we planted a crab apple seedling in front of the school. Over the years I would watch it grow as I passed by. Year after year it would grow taller and taller. The tree lived over sixty years before it was cut down.

In the third grade we were taught all about birds. We were shown beautiful pictures of the birds with the names attached. After looking and studying the birds we were given a test and I remember that I got them all right. Who ever heard of a tufted titmouse in the third grade?

In the fourth grade I got a whipping for putting a thumbtack under someone's seat. That's all I remember.

In the fifth grade we had a harvest contest. You were to bring something baked or a fruit or vegetable. I brought the biggest red delicious apples you ever laid your eyes on, and won a blue ribbon.

In science class you got extra credit for bringing in different things from the outdoors. I brought in a praying mantis cocoon. We put it in a glass cage by the window and waited. After awhile there were little praying mantis's everywhere. That spring I took in some tadpoles that I found while hunting mushrooms. We watched the tadpoles legs grow out until they were little frogs.

I had a pony when I was in the fifth grade that a man said we could have if we would give it a good home, and we did. If you had a pony back then what would you name it? That's right: Trigger. I used to jump on his back like Roy Rogers. One evening while Trigger was eating, Hickie told me to jump on his back. Trigger was a Welch pony, which are the type of ponies that are not too big or too little. I was not very tall. I proceeded to jump on his back, but didn't quite make it. As I backed up to try again, he reared up and the hoof of his hind leg caught me just above my forehead. Hickie asked me if he got me and I told him he didn't, but it sure was close. When I removed my hand from my forehead it was full of blood.

We jumped in the old 1936 Pontiac and proceeded down Main Street to Dr. Hill's office. Hickie laid on the horn all the way there. Dr. Hill sewed me up, wrapped my head in a bandage and said to come back in two weeks. I went back and he took off the bandage and felt around and told me to come back next week and we will take out the stitches. All I could think about that week was the removal of those stitches. The day came to remove the stitches. While in the doctor's office he proceeded to look at the wound and said that it was healing up nicely. He told me I could go home now, but to be careful when you are around that pony. I asked him if he was going to take out the stitches today, and he said, "Oh, I forgot. I took them out last week." I was stunned. Although the wound healed nicely, I still carry a scar today from that injury.

It was springtime and our fifth grade class played softball. I ask Dr. Hill if I could play. He asked me if I had a football helmet and I told him I did. He told me that if I'd wear my football helmet I could play softball. I played softball that year with a football helmet on. Our team went undefeated that year. Hickie made us a plaque. He stained a piece of walnut wood, and on the wood he placed shinny brass metal plates with our names on each plate. At the top of the plaque he placed a small plastic brass-colored softball that came from a penny bubble gum machine. The plaque hung in the school hall for many years. I wish I knew what happened to it.

In the sixth grade I had appendicitis about half way through. For some reason after they operated on me they put iodine all around my abdomen. I guess they did that to everybody. I remember when I went back to school the kids were curious and wanted to see my scar. I pulled my pants down far enough so they could see it and they saw the iodine all around me. Their eyes lit up and said, "What's that?" I said, "What's what?" They said, "That red stuff." I said, "Oh, that, well when you have your appendix removed the bottom half of your body turns into an Indian and you become a half-breed." They believed it until they went home and told their parents. My teacher got a kick out of it.

CONNER FARM

The Conner farm was just north of Delaware St. when Delaware Street wasn't there. The only way to get to the farm back then was a gravel road that started where the city building is now and follow along side the canal till it ended at the farm. The west fork runs through that farm. Woody Conner was the owner.

After playing ball on the ball diamond in Creitz Park on hot summer days, some of us boys would walk up the river to one of our swimming holes we called "the ledge," and swim and cool off.

My friend "Bud" could not swim and was afraid of the water, so he would sit on the bank and watch. One day the rest of us decided it was time for him to learn how to swim. We got out of the water and took him by the arms and threw him in. The water wasn't but about four foot deep so he could stand up and it would not be over his head. We made sure he wouldn't get out, so after awhile he was comfortable in the water and his fear was gone then we taught him how to swim. At our 50th high school reunion, I mentioned it to Bud and he still remembered that day. He said, "How could I forget?" Bud ended up being offensive end on the football team our senior year and was the class president, I might add, and after college went on to be a schoolteacher.

I used to help bale hay on the Conner farm in the summer. I would get a penny a bale. Some days we would put up a thousand to fifteen hundred bales that was $10.00 to $15.00 a day. Back in the 50's that was a lot of money for one day's work for a school student. When we baled we would take a break about 2:00 o'clock in the afternoon for lunch. The women would put on a feast and did we eat well. After the word got out that you were a pretty good worker other farmers would call you to help them. They would come and pick you up and take you to their farm. I would sometimes work on the wagons to load the bales, and sometimes I got to drive the tractor with a load of hay back to the barn, and boy was that fun. Other times I would work in the barns to stack. It was really hot working in the barns.

While waiting on a load of hay to come back to the barn, we would kill time by catching horse flies. Horse flies look like giant houseflies. We would catch them and take a piece of straw about five inches long, stick it up it's behind then we would launch the fly and it would go straight up in the air out of sight. The reason the fly could only go straight was the piece of straw prohibited the fly from maneuvering from one side to the other. The next time you are on a farm look for a horse fly and try it.

When the corn was ready to harvest on the Conner farm, I would sometimes go over and sit on the wagon and ride it back and forth from the field to the barn. The corncribs would have lots of mice, so I would take my BB gun and lots of times shoot at the mice.

One time I remember it was spring and Hickie and I were up the river fishing. On the way home we saw Woody Conner and his dad standing over a cow. We proceeded over to where they were and discovered the cow was trying to birth a calf but the calf was lodged and could not come out. Woody reached in to pull out both legs and managed to bring out the head and then grabbed the legs and pulled the calf the rest of the way out. I had never experienced anything like that before. It was my first experience of live birth, and a dramatic one at that, I must say.

In the summer our family would walk up the river. The cornfield was next to the river, and when the corn was ripe Hickie would pick a few ears and we would build a fire. Mom would bring along a pot. We would use the water out of the river and boil it, put the corn in and when it was cooked and ready we would have field corn on the cob. Sometimes we would just build a fire and put the corn in husks and all, and when the outside of the husks was burned black, we would take them out and feast on them.

One Sunday afternoon we had a picnic up the river, and did some fishing also. We had caught a stringer of fish and just left them in the water while we were eating and playing games.

When we were leaving, Hickie went to get the fish and as he walked over to where the fish were, a big hard- shelled turtle was sitting there in the water eating the fish. Needless to say, we had turtle to eat later on that week. All these things happened on the same river I hunted, fished, and trapped on when I was growing up on the west fork.

COON HUNTING AND TRAPPING

Raccoons are medium sized animals, 12-35+ lbs. and 20-40 inches long, including a bushy tail with 4 to 7 black rings. The fur has a tan and pepper appearance with the black mask marking on a tan face characteristic of the species. The colors can range from yellowish tan to almost black. The tracks of the raccoon are very distinctive. The hind foot is long, narrow, and rests flat on the ground like those of a bear. The front paw is hand-like, with toes that are long and well separated

Raccoons breed mainly in February and March, but matings may occur from December through June. The gestation period is about 63 days. Most litters are born in April or May, but some late-breeding females may not give birth until June, July, or August. Raccoons produce one litter per year. The average litter size is 3 to 5 young and the babies are referred to as "coon kittens." The "kittens" are weaned between 2 and 4 months of age and usually stay with the female until the following spring.

The diet of the raccoon is extremely diverse. They will eat fruit, berries, grain, eggs, poultry, vegetables nuts, fish, insects, and rodents. Individual animals may learn to use specialized foods such as poultry, fruit crops or garbage by watching other raccoons. Contrary to popular myth, raccoons do not always wash their food before eating, although they frequently play with their food in water.

In much of the U.S., raccoons are hunted for sport, and less as a food source. One reason hunters like chasing raccoons is that raccoons are a real challenge to catch. Raccoons have a bag of tricks to try to fool a hound dog and throw hounds off their trail. While being chased by hounds sniffing their trail on the ground a raccoon may enter a creek where its scent is quickly washed away, walk in the water a distance, and then escape on dry land. He might walk across a floodgate to the other side of a creek to throw off the scent. Or it might climb a tree, follow a long, low lying branch, and then jump back to the ground, trying to break up his scent trail. It might even climb a narrow fence and run along the top of the fence where the dogs can't follow. This kind of smart thinking makes many people assume that raccoons are extremely intelligent.

Many zoologists would say that a lot of what appears to be raccoon intelligence is, in fact, instinct. Breaking a scent trail by wading in a stream, or climbing a tree and jumping from a low branch, or running along the top of a narrow fence all appear to be instinctual or the innate behavior with which raccoons are born and doesn't have to be learned. It is just information carried in the animal's inherited genetic code. Whatever it is, they are "smart".

In the wild, raccoons like nothing more than a hole in a tree in which to make a den, but they also den up in holes in the ground, and rock crevices. Contrary to some beliefs, raccoons do not hibernate.

My mom dropped my dad off coon hunting one night in their model A Ford about 6 miles from their home. He was hunting on a farm just north of Cambridge City. He had an old dog that belonged to Zook before the fire by the name of Joe. Old Joe treed on this big old oak den. Coon were scarce back in the 40's. If you caught ten coons a year you had a good year.

My dad decided he was going to climb the tree. About that time it started to snow. As my dad was about 15 feet up, he slipped and fell to the ground. Upon impact he landed on his left ankle and broke it. There he was, a mile from the road with flashlight, lantern, the rifle, the dog, and one broken ankle. When he told me the story, he also taught me a valuable lesson, and that was to be extra careful and don't take chances when you are hunting alone.

Clarence Zook on the right and Hickie in the middle. 1929

Hickie and I coon hunted many woods in Western Wayne County including the canal and the West fork of the Whitewater from Cambridge City to Hagerstown. On the river we hunted the farms of Woody Conner, Paul Bertsch, Rueben Bertsch, Luther Bertsch, and Raymond Meyers. Some of the woods we hunted were Mason's, Thornburg's, Francis Duebel's, Billy Bertram's, the old Williams sisters', John Humick's, Charlie Boyd's, and Thurman Riggs, to name a few. My dad had permission to hunt everywhere he went.

My first coon dog was part black and tan and part cur. His name was Trim. I always felt that dogs with just a little cur in them made better hunters, had better noses, and treed a little harder and faster. I guess I believed that because my dad always said it. We couldn't afford a pedigreed dog anyhow, so maybe that is why we thought our dogs were better. I was twelve years old when my dad bought old Trim for me. He paid $25.00 for him and later on I was offered a cow and $200.00 for him. Obviously I turned down the offer.

I used to take old Trim to wild coon hunts. Let me explain a wild coon hunt. Back then conservation clubs would have coon hunting contests, and still do, and we would go and pay an entry fee and they would put you with three other hunters and their dogs and a judge. The judge would take us all to a woods and we would all let our dogs out.

The first dog that struck a track would get 100 points, the second dog that opened got 75 points, and 50 points for the third dog, and 25 points for the last dog if he opened. The same procedure occurred when the dogs treed. After the hunt, which was usually about 3 hours long, the dog with the most points was declared the winner of his cast. Then the second night all of the cast winners would be paired up and the highest point cast winners would be the winner of the hunt. Old Trim was a winner.

Normally we would tie our dogs to the dog box, but old Trim was different. He was somehow kind of human in some ways, I thought, so we let him run loose most of the time. He pretty much stayed around the yard unless he decided to go hunting up the canal by himself. He lived to hunt and so did I.

In the autumn you could take him squirrel hunting on a windy day and he would tree squirrels for you, which would help you spot them. Why on a windy day? Well, when it's still and the wind is not blowing the leaves on the trees you can hear a squirrel and see the limbs move when he moves. You also can hear and see them cutting on a beech, hickory, or whatever they are eating. Squirrels are harder for a hunter to hear and see when the wind blows. A lot of times the squirrel will come down from the trees to get to where they are going (particularly in the fall of the year around October when the leaves start to fall) and the dog will pick up the scent and follow it to the tree where the squirrel went up.

In November coon season would come in, and so would rabbit season. Old Trim was an unusual and unique dog, almost kind of human, I thought. You could take him rabbit hunting in the daytime, hunt him all day, and after dark go coon hunting all night and he would never run a rabbit. You might suppose that in the light of the moon he might run a rabbit, but no, not even when the moon was full. Yes, he knew what he was out there for.

Hunters used to say if a coon would get in a fight with a dog in the water, the coon would drown the dog. One night I was hunting with Trim upon West River when he hit a track. He took it across the river and treed the coon in a big willow. It was raining hard that night--I mean it was pouring down. The river was rising very fast, and it was very difficult to get across in my hip boots without going over the tops. Finally, with flashlight, lantern, and rifle, I managed to scoot across without falling down. I shined the light in the willow, and there he was on a big limb, those two old eyes shining back at me. I don't know if you have ever tried to shoot a coon out while holding the flashlight in one hand and balancing the rifle in the other hand and trying to aim at the same time. Believe me, it is not easy, and to add to all this it was pouring down rain. I was not the best shooter after dark, either. With the flashlight over my head, trying to keep a light on the coon, water dripping down from the bill of my ball hat and on to the barrel of the rifle, I managed to squeeze off a shot. With the rain coming down so hard and the tree so close to the river, I wanted to make sure I would kill the coon with one shot because I didn't want the coon to get in the water and I didn't want Trim to go in after him as I knew what the consequences might be.

Pow! Pop! I had hit the coon in the gut and he immediately headed straight down the tree. Before I knew it, Trim had grabbed the coon, and both the coon and the dog were in the water and the fight began. I was shining the light on them as the current was taking them down stream rapidly. The coon and the dog went under the water and I lost sight of them. I panicked. Was the coon going to drown my dog? I found them with the flashlight as they came to the top of the water. The coon was on top of my dog's back and I could not do anything. I felt so helpless. The only thing I could do was to say a few choice words to the coon and encourage my dog. They went under again and it seemed like they were under forever. I didn't know what to think. Had the coon drowned Trim? Was what they said true? I was getting worried about how I would explain all this to my dad. I was this 15-year old boy in which he put so much trust by letting me night hunt by myself. All of a sudden I spotted a head pop up. Was it Trim or the coon? It was Trim holding the coon in his mouth! Trim could have dropped the coon in the water after drowning it, but he didn't. He swam to the edge of the bank with the coon in his mouth. I grabbed the dog and the coon and pulled them both out of the water.

When they were out, the dog still had the coon by the throat. I know that dog thought like a human in many ways. He was definitely the smartest dog I have ever seen. I loved him very much. Ironically, this all happened on the opposite side of the river from the old oak tree where my dad fell several years ago and broke his ankle while he was coon hunting by himself. That night you could have offered me $5000.00 and a whole dairy herd of cattle for my dog and I would have said, "No thanks!" I loved that dog!

I remember one year my dad and I were hunting in Mason's woods on opening night, November 15. We owned a dog at that time in the 1950's appropriately named Elvis. Elvis was 3/4 blue tick and 1/4 cur. We got him in Kentucky. They said he had to be taken out of the state or be killed because of chasing deer. We had little, if any, deer in our eastern Indiana area back then. Once in a while you would read in the paper of a deer that strayed in front of an oncoming car and was killed and given to the county farm.

Well, we no sooner got into the woods that opening night when Elvis barked a few times and the next thing we knew he was treed. When we got to him and shined the flashlight on him he looked like a picture. His front feet were reared up on that sugar maple, his head was held straight up, and he was barking every breath. We shined the tree and there was not one, not two, not three, but four raccoons up that tree. That tree was lit up like Christmas.

We shot the coon out and started back to the car when Elvis caught a coon on the ground. We must have been a sight walking back to the car. My dad was carrying two coons, I had two, and Elvis was dragging one. My dad and I were allowed two coons per license per night and I'm still not sure whether the dog was allowed that fifth coon or not. Funny, I never did seem to remember to ask Charlie Jones, our area game warden, about that. Elvis was what we called a "still trailer", in other words, when he would get on a hot track, which is a track that the coon has just recently made, Elvis would not bark. By not barking he would come into closer contact with the coon and put him up a tree sooner, but many times he would catch them on the ground.

Uncle Jim lost his hunting license in October one year for shooting a wood duck out of season. This really put a hardship on Jim because he was a coon hunter also and the season was coming in soon. He had no license, but he had one of the best coon dogs in the area. Jim came over to the house one day. We were talking and he said, "I'll make you a bargain. You hunt my Jim dog (his coon dog was named Jim) and Elvis together.

You carry the lantern and I'll follow behind you in the dark and carry the rifle. That is the way we hunted that year from November through December.

Thanksgiving Eve we were hunting north of town close to the river. I carried the lantern and Jim followed in the dark. Old Trim hit a track and he and Jim dog worked the track for more than a mile. I kept following with the lantern and Jim kept trying to keep up in the dark. Finally, Old Trim and Jim Dog treed on a big cottonwood. I shined the tree and there he was!

Jim said, while standing back in the dark, "Do you see him?"

I said, "I sure do. Would you like to shoot him out?"

Jim replied, "I sure would!" Jim shot the coon and out he fell. It was a big black sugar coon and the biggest coon we had ever caught. We continued to hunt that way until the first of the year and then Uncle Jim got his license back. We hunted together a lot, but Uncle Jim was never in the dark after that.

Jim Dog--a Blue Tick hound

Hickie and I were hunting one November evening up on old State Road 1. We let Elvis out of the truck and was lighting the lantern when no sooner had he hit the woods than he barked a few times and treed right at the edge. We walked over to the tree. It was just a little buckeye tree and the trunk went up about twelve feet and then formed a Y and that is all there was. It was a light evening and we could see there was nothing on the tree without even shining a light. There weren't even any leaves on the tree. That dog was all over the tree, jumping up and down and would not quit barking. Hickie said he knew that coon went up that tree by the way that dog is treeing. Incidentally, there were no other trees around. It was just standing there by itself. Dad told me to climb up to the fork in the tree. I asked what for and he told me to just climb up to the fork. I climbed the tree and just as I put my hand on top of the fork of the tree, I felt hair. You would never believe it unless you were there, but there was a hole on top of the Y. The Y was no more than two fists around. There was not one, but two coons in that hole! Elvis was saying by his actions that the coon went up that tree and my dad knew Elvis was right. Sure enough, they were both right.

Shortly after high school I had to make a choice. I gave Elvis to my dear friend of many years, Smitty (Briar) Raleigh Smith; He often said Elvis was the best coon dog he had ever owned.

For 15 years, Hickie and Briar use to have an annual coon supper. I was just a young boy when they first started them. They were first held at Huber's restaurant on Main Street. At the end of the season they would sell tickets to friends and coon hunting buddies. The meal was country style. It would consist of mashed potatoes and gravy, sweet potatoes, green beans, corn, whiting fish, and, of course, baked coon. For dessert, they would have cake, pie, and Jell-O. When the women servers would have the tables all set up with food, everyone would sit down and enjoy a delicious meal.

When everyone had all they wanted to eat, the women would clear the tables. After dinner the conservation officers would have a program and speak for a while. They would share new hunting laws for the coming year. They would then have a question and answer time. They would also ask for suggestions from the hunters on hunting, trapping, and fishing. After they were finished with that part of the program the conservation officers would show a film on Indiana wild life, or something on conservation. When the program was over, Briar and Hickie would ask everyone if they had enough to eat, and thanked them for coming. Some of the men would sit down and play cards, and some would sit around and talk about their hunting experiences for the year. The men would share stories about their dogs, and how many coons they had caught that season. The supper grew to about 150 so it was moved to the American Legion building. We soon grew out of that building and moved it to Manlove Park. There we had as many as 250 coon hunters, conservation officers from several counties, and law enforcement officers, sheriff departments from several counties, and many business people. We were pretty well organized by that time. It was a great experience.

These are some of the pictures of some of the coon suppers.

Taken at Huber's Café. The two young fellows on the right side of the middle table are me and Froggie. My dad is on the left—the one with no hair. Briar is three down from my dad.

Taken at the American Legion.

This picture was taken when we moved the supper to Manlove Park.

THE RIVER

It was one hot day in July, 1948. I was 8 years old. My dad took me fishing with him that day. We had been fishing the West Fork up at Paul Bertsch's bridge. Dad was fishing a hole right below the bridge. North Simmons Creek poured into the river right below the bridge. I was tired of fishing so I started playing in the water on Simmons creek, splashing my arms and kicking my feet, when all of a sudden I was swimming. I yelled for my dad and he came over. I can still remember him sitting there on the bank watching me swim for the first time. He had the proudest look on his face. Hickie was an excellent swimmer himself and loved the water. That day he was very happy, and so was I.

Hickie would teach me things about nature when we were up the river. Some of the things he taught me were the different kinds of trees--the sycamores, the maples, the elm and the ash, the cottonwoods, hackberry, chinquapin oak, white oak, hickory, box elder, hedge apple, beech, ironwood, willow, box elder, and thorn locust. He taught me what trees the squirrels would feed or (cut) on, and when it was the right time for each tree to produce food.

We had all kinds of flowers like white, pink, yellow, and purple violets and beautiful bluebells. I used to pick my mom bouquets of bluebells. By the time I would carry them all the way back home they would wilt, but she would put them in water and they would look good and fresh. There used to be lots of wild roses in white and pink and the petals were smaller than the tame roses.

Springtime would bring up the May apples and other woods greenery like sweet anise. When I would be hunting mushrooms and get a little thirsty I would pull up some anise and chew on it and it would quench my thirst. West River was a fun place to be. Being close to the river and loving nature meant I spent a lot of time on the West Fork.

The Sears Roebuck & Co. (known today as Sears) was one of the largest fur buying companies in North America. They started buying furs in 1925 establishing 8 fur-receiving depots throughout the USA. For 35 years Sears successfully marketed trapping supplies and furs

To promote their fur marketing, Sears created a booklet and called it "Sears Tips to Trappers" by Johnny Muskrat! Johnny Muskrat was Sears's spokesperson that edited the booklet and narrated the weekly fur market broadcast from WLS (World's Largest Store) radio station in Chicago.

Sears also hosted the annual "National Fur Show" from 1926 through 1958, which awarded top prizes to trappers. Awards were given for the best pelt handling, which included a new Plymouth automobile. In 1959 Sears decided to stop buying furs. It was that year that the company changed their merchandising strategy from rural America to the urban market. Unfortunately, Hickie and I were never awarded a prize.

Maas & Steffen Inc., located in St. Louis, Missouri, was one of the powerhouses in the early fur market. St. Louis was the fur capital of North America at the time. The Corporation started buying fur in the early 1900's. Maas & Steffen Inc. advertised with colorful trapping supply catalogs, posters, envelopes and calendars. No other fur company could match their large lithographic colored pictorial calendars.

Setting a trap line on the west fork was a learning and profitable experience and Hickie was an experienced trapper and knew a lot about trapping different animals. He grew up trapping muskrats, mink, and raccoon. After catching one of these animals in his trap, he would bring it home and skin it out, turn the fur inside out, and stretch it on a fur board. He had different sizes of fur boards—one size for muskrats, one size for mink, and another size for raccoon.

When you skinned a fur and stretched the hide inside out and scraped the excess fat from it, you would hang it up to dry and then at the end of the season you would take the furs off the boards, take them to the fur buyer, and sell them. We would sell a lot of our furs right before Christmas. The money came in handy.

Most everyone knew that Hickie was an avid hunter, fisherman, and trapper, and realized his knowledge of animals and the outdoors. One day we got a call from one of dad's friends, Harvey Bertsch, who owned a farm just north of Germantown on the Germantown road. Mr. Bertsch trapped some on the Martindale creek, which ran through his land. He said, "Hickie, I have caught something in one of my traps and I am not sure I know what it is. Can you come over and take a look at it and see if you can identify it?"

Hickie and I jumped in the car and drove over to his place. When we arrived he took us to the barn, and there was this animal that resembled a raccoon in color. It had similar markings, but it had a short tail, short legs, and long claws. My dad took one look at it and realized that it was a badger. Badgers are animals that normally live in more northern states like, Wisconsin, Minnesota, and places farther north. No one had ever heard of a badger being seen in this area, and no one has ever seen or trapped one since, as far as I know.

There have been Beavers seen and trapped in our area for many years. As a matter of fact, we were fishing Lake Wehi one evening, and all of a sudden we heard this k-plunk in the water. It sounded like someone had thrown in a boulder. Hickie thought it was probably some kids. Again, k-plunk! This time he yelled out, "Who ever you are you had better stop throwing rocks or I'm going to get out of this boat and come after you!"

About that time a beaver came up out of the water and k-plunk, as to let us know we were in his territory. Boy, did we feel embarrassed and surprised. That was our first encounter with a beaver in our area. The beavers got so bad about killing the trees around the lake that they had to be trapped.

Hickie started teaching me how to trap when I was 10. About a week or two before the season would come in we would walk the river looking for signs of muskrats, mink, and raccoon. Muskrats live in burrows in the water. When they come out of the burrow they slide in and out of the water to feed. We would walk the bank of the river looking for muskrat slides so we would know where to place our traps.

Mink like to play along drifts in the river. They also like to run in and out of the tile ditches. We would look for footprints and mink droppings. Once we found a favorite mink hangout and when the season came in we would set our traps in a likely spot in the water and never get close to that area after that.

Mink are very shy and sensitive to smell. They will shy away from man if they continually pick up his scent. We would always check a mink trap from the opposite side of the river. By doing this we kept our scent away from the trap. Mink are notorious for biting off their foot if caught in a trap. Sometimes when you checked your trap all you would have is a couple toes or a foot.

When we set a trap for a mink, we would make a set at the edge of the water, stack 2 or 3 rocks very carefully on top of each other, and place the trap on top of the rocks so that the top of the trap was just about an inch under the water to hide the chain. When a mink would get caught, he would knock the trap off the rocks and the weight of the trap would pull the mink under the water and drown him. The old trappers knew that secret about trapping for mink. We usually caught 3 or 4 mink a year and that was a good year. My dad was so good about skinning and stretching his furs that a tailor of fur coats in Connersville, Indiana, would buy our mink and pay top money.

Raccoons also like the drifts along the river as one of their favorite places. Coon run in and out of the tile ditches also, and have similar tendencies when caught in a trap. They will also bite their foot off in an effort to escape.

After we had made our trap run we would wait for the season to come in. On opening day we would count the number of traps we needed, add a few more, and take off up the river to set them. Trapping season would open in mid-November and close January 31.

You were expected to run your trap line once every 24 hours. I would get up at 4 a.m. in the morning and run my trap line, come back home, and get ready for school. In the winter months I would play basketball. Many times I would run my traps after basketball practice. I coon hunted the river a lot; so I would run my traps and coon hunt at the same time.

One time, on a Saturday morning, Hickie was helping me run the trap line. We had had a pretty good catch so far that morning. We had gotten out of the water and were walking the path to our next traps when my dad heard voices. We were on a high bank looking down into the water, and to our amazement we saw two men coming down the river running our trap line. The men didn't see us. We always carried a rifle with us when running traps.

Hickie said, "Lay down, I'm going to teach these two a lesson!"

The men kept getting closer until they were right below us. Hickie started firing shots in the water all around them. He told them to get out of the water on the other side of the river and drop the bag they were carrying to the ground, and then start running across the field on the other side of the river and don't stop.

I'll never forget them saying, "Don't shoot, don't shoot, we're sorry, don't shoot us, Hickie!"

They dropped the bag and began to run until they were out of sight. They never saw my dad or me, but they knew with whom they were dealing. After they were gone, my dad said, "Now go over and get your fur." There were six muskrats in the bag. My dad later told me those two men were known for running other men's trap lines and stealing their furs out of the traps and resetting them like nothing ever happened.

One day, my dad, my grandpa, and I were taking some furs to New Castle to be sold. We sold our muskrats and coon to Mr. Yoss, who had a fur barn on Route 3 North across from the American Legion Golf Course. We had turned off on the wrong street in New Castle and my dad ran a stop street accidentally. The police about a block down the road stopped us. The policeman gave my dad a ticket for running the stop street and told him to be careful. We got back on the right road and found our way to Mr. Yoss' fur barn.

As always, Mr. Yoss was glad to see us. He gave us a cup of coffee and proceeded to look at our furs. He paid my dad $36.00 for our furs and we left and drove back home. Later the next week, Dad had to drive back to new Castle and pay his fine. The fine cost him exactly $36.00.

I used to have a few traps set in a pond north of town and my dad would drive me there and I would run the traps and stay there awhile and duck hunt. It was time to quit hunting. I started walking back to the car when a big star skunk ran across my path. It was my first encounter with a skunk in broad daylight. You could always smell skunks but very rarely see them. Anyhow, there he was. I knew a star skunk was worth $1.50 and that was pretty good. Considering I caught nothing in my traps and no ducks, I thought that if I shot him that the day wouldn't be a total loss. I got a little closer to him and unloaded on him with my 12 gauge. I waited a minute or two to see if there was any odor before I picked him up. I couldn't smell a thing, so I picked him up and headed back to the auto to show off my first skunk to my dad. As I was walking, I began to smell a small odor. I thought it was no big deal. It's a skunk and it's only normal to smell a little. As I walked a little further, the smell began to get a little stronger. By the time I was about two thirds of the way to the auto, I let the skunk kind of just slide out of my hand, as the smell was so strong it was making tears come out of my eyes. When I got back to the auto, my dad was standing outside.

He said one thing. "You are walking home. There is no way you are getting in this car smelling like that!"

After telling him my story with tears in my eyes and feeling very sickly, his compassion came through. Only after taking all my clothes off and putting them in the trunk, wrapping in a blanket we had in the car, was I able to ride home. He showed compassion, but boy was he mad!

A couple of days later I picked the skunk up, put him in a burlap sack and we went and sold him. When I told the fur buyer the story he thought it was so funny he gave me $2.00. Yes, the story stinks, but the outcome was kind of sweet.

One evening after school when I was running my traps, I kept smelling oil fumes all the way up the river. Hickie was to meet me at Paul Bertsch's bridge. Before I got to the bridge, oil started flowing down the water and I wondered what had happened. When I got to the bridge, Hickie and two game wardens were standing on the bridge looking at the crude oil that had covered the whole river. Charlie Jones and Dale Hood, the wardens, were so mad that one of them threw his cigarette into the oil hoping to set it on fire. Lucky for him, it didn't.

What had happened was that an oil pipeline had burst up near Hagerstown and the oil had spilled into the river. I could understand why the wardens were mad and so were Hickie and I because we were all afraid that the oil would kill the fish and all the animals that used the river. It took several days for the oil to move on down the river. It still had left several potholes covered with oil. Hickie and I would go up the river and he would set some of the pothole on fire and burn off the oil.

Froggie and I were up the river one day and on the way home we noticed a pothole had formed around one of the supports on the new bridge on Delaware Street. Froggie and I knew Hickie had been burning the oil off of potholes and we decided to help him out by burning the oil off this one. We set it on fire and the flames and smoke kept spreading. What we didn't know was that the potholes that Hickie burned had water under them and he could control the flames by throwing a log on them and the water would splash up and control the fire. The pothole that we were burning was pure oil, so when we threw a log on the flames it would just spread the fire.

After a while we heard the fire sirens start blowing and it didn't take long to figure out why. I headed west and Froggie headed south. I changed my clothes and went back to the bridge. The bridge contractor that built the bridge was there as well as the fire department. It didn't take any time to put out the fire because they had water. The contractor said the fire took fifty years off the life of the bridge. That was over fifty-five years ago. Froggie and I promised not to ever tell anyone, and as far as I know I have just broken that promise. Sorry Froggie!

SQUIRREL HUNTING

Hickie and I were squirrel hunting in Golay's woods. Before we started hunting he told me there were cattle in the woods, but they would be of no bother. The design of the woods was a box L shape. In the front part of the woods you walked through a field and then entered the woods. At the back end of the woods you walked directly into the woods after you went over the fence. The back part is where we chose to enter. After we entered the woods we split up.

I was in the woods about two hours or so and had killed three squirrels when I noticed the cattle. Hickie also told me there might be a bull in their midst. The cows saw me and started walking my direction. They then started running toward me. Well, I didn't sit there; I jumped up and took off with a run of my own right toward the car. I thought the car was at the edge of the woods, which it was when I started, but I had worked my way to the front of the woods.

To my surprise at the end of the woods there was no fence. I said, "Oh no!" There I was with the shotgun in one hand three squirrels in the other, legs feeling pretty flimsy, and the cattle on my heels. I ran so fast that when I got to that fence I believe I hurdled over it. The cattle stopped at the fence and just stood there and looked at me, as if to say, "It was just a game, chump!" Stupid beasts! I caught my breath for a minute and walked back to the car.

Hickie finally came out of the woods carrying his limit of squirrels and asked if everything was all right. I said, "Yea, now it is!" He said, "What do you mean?" I told him I just got run out of the woods by a bunch of cattle. Of course he laughed, as I knew he would. I kind of laughed to. Then he told me that all I had to do was stop running and they would too. They were just playing. FAT CHANCE.

MUSHROOM SEASON

Every year the Hicks family would go mushroom hunting. We each had our own hunting grounds. My uncles, my dad and I would start hunting around the middle of April until the second week of May. We would mainly look for the morel sponge mushrooms. Hickie taught me that when hunting mushrooms you walk very slowly and look around all the trees where they might be. Sometimes when you find one there is usually another one close by. Many times you find them in a bunch.

In late March and early April we would start finding the black sponges. In our area they grow mostly around the wild cherry trees and pine trees and are very difficult to see. Sometimes we would get on our hands and knees to find the blacks. Blacks can be very tall also. About the same time in early April the gray sponge start popping up. They grow around the ash, elm, and apple trees. The spikes, as we called them, like to come up after a good rain and you might find them anywhere, and especially among the May apples. The spike, snakehead, or peckerhead as some call them is a little different in their shape. The spike has a long, light-colored stem with a smaller brown head. You have to be careful in the way you handle them, because they are more fragile and not as firm as the morels.

The big yellow sponge usually comes up last. They like to grow around old elm snags and ash trees. They also grow around sycamores and in pastures around wild rose bushes. The yellow sponge can grow from 5 to 15 inches. We always got permission from the landowner when we hunted mushrooms.

I guess I had found a half a sack of mushrooms one time when we were hunting up north of town, when all of a sudden I heard a rustling in a tree above me. As I took my eyes from the ground and looked up I was amazed to see a huge black snake making a nest in a hollow place in the tree. I thought that it was very unusual. I had never seen anything like this before. As I stopped to watch, it went about arranging the weeds, which evidently a bird had left to make a nest. Finally it finished and went inside and curled up as if it was satisfied. After that little episode I couldn't help but look for snakes as well as mushrooms.

A couple of other things you have to watch for in the woods are foxes and skunks that might be rabid. An animal that is not walking normally or walking with a swagger and foaming at the mouth may well have rabies. My dad actually had to kill a young rabid fox.

Springtime is so beautiful in Indiana. After a long winter all the wild flowers start to pop up. The trees are all budded out. This used to be an old saying: *The dogwoods are in bloom with blossoms, like the cross for all to see. As blood stains the petals marked in brown, the blossom's center wears a thorny crown. All who see it will remember me. Crucified on a cross from a dogwood tree.* Certainly the dogwood tree in blossom is a beautiful sight. The red buds accent the woods with a lavender touch. This small, sparsely branched tree also is called the Judas tree, and is said by some to be the one from which Judas Iscariot hanged himself after betraying Christ.

There is nothing any more rewarding than walking out of the woods with a big mess of morel mushrooms. After we would bring our mushrooms home, Hickie would run them under the water faucet and cut them in half and clean the bugs out. Then they were soaked in salt water to further remove the bugs. After soaking, they were drained and put in the refrigerator. Sometimes we would clean them and have some for dinner. My mom would roll them in flour and fry them in butter. Boy they were good, and still are. My uncle Dave would sometimes find the biggest one of the year. I have included a picture of some that he found and we found.

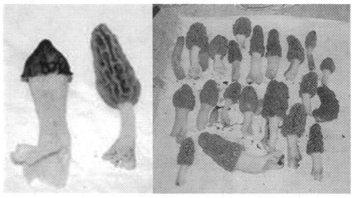

Spike on the left , the rest yellow sponge

Mess of sponge.

2--National Road Traveler   May 13, 1981

'raveler
15c
per copy

Cambridge City, Indiana

MUSHROOMS, ANYBODY?--David Hicks proudly displays a few of the bigger mushrooms he found last week "north of Cambridge City". The biggest of the group weighed three fourths of a pound, measured 13 inches tall and 13½ inches in circumference.

NRT Photo

Uncle Dave and a couple of whoppers

NATIONAL ROAD U.S. 40

U.S. 40 highway extends from Atlantic City, New Jersey, West, to Park City, Utah. At it's beginning it extended across the entire U.S. Before Interstate 70, everyone who was traveling by automobile had to drive through Cambridge City, Indiana. It was always fun to look at the license plates from different states. It didn't make any difference who you were, if you were traveling east or west, on U.S.40 you had to go through our town. President Truman came through here. One time Roy Rogers traveled through town. Gene Autry came here to look at a horse one of the town's people owned.

The Indianapolis 500 race was run every Memorial Day when I was growing up. All of the cars going east had to pass through town. After the race ended, Hickie and I would walk down to U.S. 40, sit on the steps of Maloney's grocery store, and wait on the cars to come back east. As they came I would count the Fords and he would count the Chevrolets. There were cars from Ohio, Pennsylvania, New Jersey, New York, Maryland, Virginia, West Virginia, and others. People from all over the United States would attend the Indianapolis 500; after all, it is the greatest spectacle in racing.

Not only did all the autos have to pass through town on U. S. 40, but they also stopped and purchased goods. All the stores were doing well and more and more stores were opening new businesses.

We had a hardware-grocery store owned by the Omit Brothers. Grandma would order her groceries and they would home deliver in their little Ford truck. I remember they had wooden bushel baskets. Each basket had a different kind of nut in it. One would have peanuts, another pecans, another English walnuts, almonds, hazel nuts, Brazil nuts, and others. One day when I was about six I went with her, and as she was shopping I went over to where the nuts were and filled my pocket full of English walnuts. When she had finished her shopping she noticed my pocket was bulging out. She asked me what was in my pocket, and I told her, "Walnuts." Back to the store we went, and right in front of everyone I had to empty my pocket. Boy was that humiliating, but a lesson learned.

Another business I remember was Brunner's Drug store. Dale Brunner owned the store. In the store was a soda fountain, bar and stools, just like in the movies. I went to school with one of his daughters. Mr. Brunner was a nice gentleman. I always thought he looked like a movie star, with wavy hair and his kind manner.

Then there was Mr. Henderson, of Henderson's clothing. He always had a half chewed cigar hanging out of his mouth. He was another wonderful man. Each year when trapping season came in, I would go down to their store, ask for him, and he would come out and greet me and say, "It must be trapping season!" He would put his arm around my shoulder and take me over to the hip boot area and fit me with a new pair of Red Ball hip boots. He would then give me a bill, and tell me I could pay him when I caught some muskrats. I paid him every year. Mr. Henderson was a good man.

Other stores included Danners Dime Store, The Western Auto store, Huber's Café, and Daisy Diamond's Restaurant, Les Doniker's filling station, and Bill Close's filling station.

When Interstate 70 was built, it took a lot of business away from our town and all of the small towns in America along U. S. 40 Highway. The interstate system forever changed the America that we once knew.

CREITZ PARK

The Cambridge City Tribune on July 2, 1925 announced and advertised Creitz Park's formal opening. Cambridge City's town park was given its official name in 1925, seventeen years after it's original purchase. On July the fourth of that year the town's people held an official opening of the naming of Creitz Park. Electrical lights were installed, flower gardens were planted, and a well was dug to supply drinking water. Dozens of tables and benches were added. There was a Band concert, singing, and various talks. Folks came and brought their picnic baskets and made a day out of it. There was also a swimming area constructed in the river. Damming the river created it. The east side of the swimming area had a sandy beach, and the west side had steps leading down to the water. Two bathhouses were constructed. The swimming area was 100 ft. long and 40 ft. wide, and was positioned at the approximate location of the swinging bridge

It was May and school was just over for the summer. For several summers my older sister, brother, little sister and I would go to the park and clean out the swimming pool. This pool was made of cement and was round in shape and about 20 ft. in diameter and was about 30 inches deep, as I recall. After we had it clean, Tink Babinger, who helped take care of

The swinging bridge

the park, would come over and turn on the water. After the pool had been filled we would play in it all day long. Boy, was it freezing cold! After a day or two of warm weather, the water in the pool would warm up. The word was soon out that the pool was filled with water and kids came from all over town to play in the pool. We had swings, and a merry-go-round, shuffleboard courts, horseshoe courts, picnic tables, and later on a basketball court, and an outdoor skating rink.

Pete Murley would come over with a crane shortly after school was out for the summer and dig out a swimming hole for the older kids in the Whitewater just above the swinging bridge. When I was not too much older I, too, would swim there and swing out over the water off of the grape vines. We had no idea that there was once a swimming hole that was dug out some 25 to 30 years earlier.

Pete Murley was one of the best heavy equipment operators around. He owned the only pay fishing pond in the area after WWII. He and his wife and two daughters lived south of Milton about two miles on Indiana 1. Down the hill below the house he had three fishing ponds that were called G&G lakes. The ponds were full of catfish and carp and Pete would charge people to fish in them. The ponds are still there and still called G & G lakes.

Later he drudged out the lakes in Mt. Auburn behind what use to be the K & J drive-in, and made more pay fishing ponds, now called Highway Springs, and in the middle pond we used to swim and dive in. He then drudged out the lake at Lake View Restaurant. Later he drudged the twin lakes on U.S. 40 over by poor farm hill near Centerville. He also dug out the ponds at Doc-o-Lakes on Pennville road south.

Maynard Wolf started a summer program at Creitz Park. Mr. Wolf as we called him, was the Lincoln High School Principal at that time. The summer program was for both boys and girls. There were contests for shuffleboard, badminton, horseshoe, and other activities.

Morning little league baseball was really big when we were growing up. We had several teams. The teams were coached by some of the older boys. Mr. Wolf ran the whole program and it was a huge success. When we were older we moved up to the evening baseball league. My Dad coached evening baseball for over 30 years. Many kids that grew up in Cambridge City had "Hickie" for their coach.

It was late fall I was about 9 years old. My Dad and I were sucker fishing up the river above Woody Conner's farm. On the way home we stopped at the ball diamond in Creitz Park where my uncle Jim's high school team was practicing. Uncle Jim was a very good left-handed pitcher and later had a tryout with the Chicago Cubs. Back then Cambridge City didn't have football so they played baseball in the fall.

We sat down on the bench and watched them practice for a while. As I sat there I noticed a pouch of Bag Pipe chewing tobacco. Back then the boys on the ball team were allowed to chew, so when we got ready to leave I picked up the Bag Pipe and took it with me. I wanted to be like the big boys.

On the way home through the old canal as I followed my dad, I would put some in my mouth and chew it. I didn't know you were not supposed to swallow it. By the time we got home I was as sick as a dog. My mom ask my dad what was wrong with me, and of course he had no idea, until I started bringing it up. I guess I threw up so much my face turned green--or almost.

When I was in high school we played all of our home baseball games at the ball diamond in Creitz Park. We played baseball in the spring since we had football in the fall. We played all of our American Legion games there as well. We had a good baseball season my senior year 1958. We played Richmond, our county seat, population of around 35,000, that year and beat them 5 to 3 at Richmond's McBride stadium. Back then it was called the Green Fence. Richmond went on that year to a perfect record in the North Central Conference, which was the biggest and toughest conference in the state of Indiana, and won it. They also won every game that year except one. Yep, that's right, we beat them on their own turf. Cambridge City population back then was 2200. By the way, in my senior year we set the high school football record for the most wins and it has never been broken and that was the 1957- 58 season.

Growing up we were privileged to have an outside skating rink at the park. The floor was cement and it had an iron railing around it. Outside the railing were benches to sit on. After the newness wore off, the floor was like a piece of glass. If you were lucky, you had a pair of shoe skates. In the evenings the rink was full of kids, not only from Cambridge, but also from surrounding towns. Adults would drive their cars to the rink early to make sure they got a good spot to watch all the action. There was an adult who policed the rink and you didn't want to cause a commotion or you were done for the night.

There was a concession stand to purchase soft drinks, popcorn, and candy, all for 5 cents each. Someone was in the concession stand that took care of all of the music. There were all kinds of different ways to skate. There was all skate, then they would announce certain age groups only, then girls only, and then boy's only, then couples only. Then they would put out barrels at one end and the other and have races. I must say I won a few. For many of us, when you were not playing baseball in the evening you were roller-skating.

FISHING THE CREEKS

It was an overcast and rainy day, but my dad wanted to go fishing, so he took me and I took my friend, Froggie. We drove down to the Milton Bridge and he went up the creek and Froggie and I went down the creek. The creek was muddy and it started to rain, so Froggie and I headed back to the 1949 Belair.

Froggie had been allowed to smoke at home in front of his mom and grandmother, but his father, who was the local town marshal, would not allow him to smoke and didn't know he did. We were settled down in the back seat with our feet propped up on the back of the front seat, windows half way down, raining outside, and Froggie said, "Do you want a cigarette?"

I said, "Sure!" And we sat there smoking in the back seat, back windows down, smoke rolling out the windows, and having a big time. Suddenly, Hickie appeared through the weeds, catching us red-handed, as they say. Hickie made us get out of the car, took his belt off, and gave me a few good licks, then approached Froggie and said, "You're next!"

Froggie said, "You can't whip me, I'll tell my dad and have him arrest you!" Well, my dad and Froggie's dad grew up together and were good friends just as Froggie and I were.

My dad looked at Froggie and smiled. "That's just what I want you to do!" Froggie was between a rock and a hard spot, nowhere to turn, no defense, and so he got his whipping that day also. I believe that was the only whipping Froggie had ever received. Whippings with a belt sure do smart when your pants are wet from wading in the creek, but one thing for sure--you don't soon forget.

Dad, Froggie, and I went fishing one day on Martindale creek north of Germantown about four miles on Paul Worl's farm. It really wasn't a good day, because the water was murky. Froggie used to say, "Little bait--big fish." I had a little peeler crawl I put on and dropped it in the murky water just over the edge of a log. After a moment or so I started to pull my line out of the water but it wouldn't budge. When fishing in the creeks it's easy to get hung up, so I didn't think much of it. I waited a few seconds and tried to pull it up again when my line took off out from under that log. I jerked and boy was I in for a big surprise. The result was a 3 1/2 pound small-mouth bass, the biggest one I had ever caught. I was so proud. Froggie was right: little bait--big fish.

There was a gravel pit on the north side of US 40 and just east of Martindale Creek. There were several small pits and one big pit. Dad and I used to fish there. The big pit had several big bass in it. One day we were fishing there and I Hickie was using a soft craw. We used casting reels then with cloth line called camouflage. Camouflage line was supposed be transparent to the fish. Hickie would cast out and let the bait fall to the bottom and then with his fingers slowly work the line in, when you felt a tug on the line you stopped. The fish would then run with the bait until all the line was out and then when the line was tight you would jerk. As that happened, Hickie jerked and after reeling and wearing down the fish, he landed it. The result was a six and one half pound largemouth bass. My youngest son and I walked over there awhile back and there is no sign of any of the gravel pits. What a shame.

There was a restaurant called the Green Chicken on the north side of Main Street in the middle of town. Ray Moore was the proprietor and he was also the Justice of the Peace. We were in the restaurant one evening eating and talking, and Mr. Moore said he had never eaten carp and someone told him that Hickie knew how to clean a carp. Mr. Moore said you catch and clean the carp and I'll prepare them, and after I close up we will have a carp dinner. Hickie agreed.

Martindale creek was beside those gravel pits. There was a nice hole of water just north of US 40 Bridge. One winter night when the water was clear, Hickie and I and my uncle Dave took a little boat there to gig carp. We gigged eight carp that weighed a total of over one hundred pounds. Hickie cleaned them, and took them to Ray Moore who prepared some of them and froze the rest. Along with some other people, including the city police and some state police officers, we had a carp dinner.

Hickie and I would go to the Green Chicken back then for breakfast, order two eggs, hash browns, bacon, toast, and coffee for .49 cents. After the basketball games people would flock in the Green Chicken. I would order a hamburger, a bowl of chili, and a Coke for .50 cents. That place was jammed packed full of people, I mean wall-to-wall, elbowroom only. It was the place to go after the games and to hear what the downtown coaches had to say, as well as just the place to assemble. We had some excellent basketball teams in the early fifties. One of the basketball teams had a perfect twenty game winning streak.

We used to fish the creeks a lot. One Saturday my dad and I, along with "Briar"—who was like an uncle to me—were fishing below the Milton Bridge down on Cold Springs We were using soft crawls and peelers for bait. Soft crawls and peelers are crawfish. A soft crawl is one that has just shed its hard shell like when a snake sheds its skin. After it sheds its hard shell it is very soft. A peeler is a crawler that is just about ready to shed its shell, but hasn't, so you help it along by peeling it. They both are excellent small mouth bass bait.

Back then we fished in blue jeans and tennis shoes and waded the creek. Someone usually carried the hooks and one would carry the bait bucket. Whenever we came upon a ripple in the water we would look for bait also. When we caught two or three craws we would just put them in our ball hat and put the cap back on our head. Often times the peelers would peel from the heat inside the ball hat. We each had a stringer which was a piece of chalk line about 4 foot long with a stick tied on one end and the other end tied to your belt.

It just so happened that I was carrying the hooks that day and was in water up to my waist, fishing this nice hole of water and getting a bite when Briar came over to where I was and said, "I need a hook." It was not hard to lose a hook fishing the creek and drifts. Whenever he would carry the hooks he would always make you wait until he had finished the hole he was fishing.

I said, "Wait a minute, I have a bite!"

Briar said, "You ain't got no bite! Throw me the hooks!"

"Wait just a minute!" I yelled back.

All of a sudden Briar yelled out, "Son, I kid you not, there's a big snake coming right at you!"

I thought, 'Yeah, he just wants a hook and he's getting impatient. Well, he can just wait! I have a bite!'

Again he yelled, "Son, I'm not kidding, there's a big snake coming right towards you!"

When he said son, I decided to look, and sure enough, here came this big snake swimming right toward me! I'm in water up to my waist with sand under my feet, so I can't move very fast and that thing is coming right at me within maybe six feet. It was the biggest water snake I had ever seen—maybe five to six feet long. By this time Briar is throwing rocks at it and I am trying to hit it with my fishing pole and not moving too fast in that sandy bottom. It must have seen me at that point, because in an instant it stopped. Its head literally came out of the water about two feet. It's head then spread out like a cobra and sat there. It literally sat up in the water and never moved. At that point I didn't know what it was going to do. We were shocked, and I kept swatting my pole at it and yelling, finally, it swam over to the other side and went up and incline bank.

As I made it out of the water, Briar and I in our excitement said that it looked like a cobra. With all the yelling and commotion, my dad came running over to us and asked what was going on. When we told him the story, he said it was probably a spreading viper. What ever it was I was glad it went up the bank rather than coming after me.

LAKE WEHI

Hickie used to box—all five feet three and one-half inches of him. They used to call him "Kid Hicks." He would fight his bouts at a beautiful lake we were blessed to have in our area named Lake Wehi. The late, great Jack Dempsey refereed one of his fights.

The **Palladium-Item** headlines read: *WEHI BOXING AND WRESTLING CLOSED WITH A BANG ON LABOR DAY*

"The Wehi baseball team didn't make any records over Labor Day, having lost three in a row after some disastrous breaks, but the boxing and wrestling card last Monday night was a real one, and the crowd was even larger than the one last year for the bathing beauty contest. They came early and stayed late, and were afforded real entertainment. This was probably the last of the series of athletic exhibitions for this summer."

"Kid Hicks' of Pershing (East Germantown) and 'Johnny Locke' of Milton staged the opener, a 3-round whirlwind affair which was fought to a draw the best and fastest contest of the summer by far. Each was the aggressor and each carried a crimson beak at the close and each was tottering. They figured three rounds would have to be fought hard to use up all their energy, and fight

71

they did, with honors even. The crowd applauded their gameness again and again."

"Pat' Gamp of Richmond, 1927 state YMCA champion took two falls over Ivan Kossack of New York, formerly Howard Hosbrook of Richmond, who is no mean wrestler. They showed all the tricks in the trade, and were in earnest at every stage of the game, well matched. This was one of the best wrestling exhibitions seen in eastern Indiana for many years."

"The WEHI park management will probably continue the boxing and wrestling exhibitions next year, as they have proved a real card during 1932."

Lake Wehi was certainly the place to be in the summer months if you lived in and around Wayne County. There was picnicking, hiking around the lake, fishing, and, I might add, some of the best bass fishing in the area. There was boating and swimming. The lake was spring fed and the water was crystal clear. There were bathhouses for the swimmers, a concession stand, and a huge dance floor.

I don't remember too much of the dancing, but I can remember the juke box playing all day long as my dad and I were on the lake fishing. I can still hear Nat King Cole singing "Ramblin Rose" and Frankie Lane's "Mule Train," and songs like the "Yellow Rose of Texas," and the big band music with the Dorsey Brothers, and Harry James' trumpet echoing across the lake in the late afternoon or Glen Miller with his big band sound.

On Sunday afternoons in the summer they would sometimes have speed boat races with little hydroplane speedboats. The speedboats were all colors of red, green, yellow, blue, and many other colors. During race day was the only time they would allow motors on the lake. The only boats that were allowed on the lake were rowboats with oars. People from all around would come to watch the races. Mr. Wickes' son, Robert, had one of the boats that would enter in the races and he won his share.

Bass fishing season used to come in on June 15th at midnight every year. I can remember all the boats would be lined up on the shore waiting for the shotgun start at 12:00 midnight. When the gun went off, everyone jumped in their boats and headed for their favorite fishing spot. Back in those days, casting reels were the thing. If you had a Shakespeare Wonder Rod and reel, or a Pfluger Supreme, or a Heddon Pal, you had the Cadillac of fishing equipment.

I can remember the sounds of the jitterbugs as they skimmed across the top of the water, and the sound of the crazy crawler skidding across the top. The crazy crawler had to be the noisiest plug ever made, but it caught fish. Then there were the Hula Poppers popping. With all the noise it is a wonder that anybody could catch a fish. Someone would catch a bass and everyone would shine a flashlight on that boat. That whole place would light up like a Christmas tree. The light would reflect off the boat onto the water and other boats. It was a sight to behold, but we did manage to catch fish and have a fun time doing it.

The lake was full of fish. There were bigmouth bass, big bluegill, big white and black crappies, and yellow perch. I am reminded of the time my dad and I were fishing one afternoon for yellow perch. We were fishing with peelers, which are crawfish right before they molt and shed their shell. Well, that day we caught a mess of perch and I caught one that was 17 ½ inches and another one 19 ½ inches. Mr. and Mrs. Sourbeer were sitting on the bank that afternoon and saw me catch both fish. "Spin", as my dad called Mr. Sourbeer, said, "That's the biggest one I have ever seen. It must be a record. We didn't know it then, but later we found out that it would have been a state record.

My dad did hold the state record for a while for the biggest rock bass, or 'goggle eye' as we used to call them. It was caught in the West Fork. Several years later the Indianapolis Star use to have a contest every year for the biggest fish in different categories, and my dad would always catch the record yellow perch in the state and every year he would take his record catch out of Lake Wehi.

Every spring the hard shell snapping turtles would come out of hibernation. Dad and I would get in a boat and scan the lake looking for a turtle with his head stuck out of the water. After seeing one we would ease over to where it would submerge. My dad made a big hook that was fastened to a 12-foot wooden pole. He would ease the pole down slowly under the shell of the turtle and yank up on it and pull the turtle out of the water. Sometimes we would have 4 or 5 turtles in the boat at the same time, and boy would I get a little nervous.

After taking our quota home, Hickie would clean them. He would first put them in boiling water and that would remove all of the old skin and then he would cut around the underneath side of the shell and cut out piece by piece. Some of the turtles would have eggs in them. Dad would set them out to dry and later give them to us kids and we would bounce them around like ping pong balls.

Everyone went swimming at Lake Wehi. The oldest Wickes son, David, ran all the activities when I was growing up. We swam most days that the swimming area was open. Sometimes on rainy days us kids would wait all day for the rain to stop so we could go in swimming. In the swimming area there was a cement platform and on the platform there were three diving boards at different heights. The low board was about 5 ft. off the water, and then to the side of it was the second board, which was about 15 ft. from the water. The high board was about 30 ft. from the top of the water. It was a big accomplishment when you graduated to a dive from the high board.

When my dad's generation was young, they drove spikes in the light pole about 12 ft. above the high board and would dive from it. My dad was a certified lifeguard at Wehi for many years. He taught many people how to swim, and also saved many people from drowning. He was an excellent diver and could do many different dives. I used to love to watch him dive.

*The Wickes Family: Mr. & Mrs. Edwin Wickes,
David, Robert, Maxine, & Lloyd*

The bathhouse, dance hall and concessions stand in wintertime

Good For
FREE SWIM
LAKE WEHI
1937

Free swim ticket

25-cent ticket

LAKE WEHI

¼ mile south of Pershing, 2 miles east of Cambridge City

Good Fishing	Fine Swimming
Boating	Camping

Summer Cottages with Electric Lights
Tennis Court—Horseshoe Court
Ball Diamond—Croquet Court
Miniature Golf Court
Just off Concrete Road—Plenty of Free Parking
Picnic Tables—Good Drinking Water

For reservations phone 8028 or write LAKE WEHI COMPANY, Cambridge City, Indiana.

Wehi Business Card

North side of the dance hall and swimming area

Summertime swimming at Wehi in 1930.

Boat area in the 30's. The boat says Cambridge City,
but Wehi is actually in Germantown

Huge slide and the fishing boats

For several years Wehi was a very poplar resort to go to in the summer. There was entertainment for the whole family. Factories would hold their annual employee family reunions at the lake. Unfortunatly it was closed down in 1952 because of high insurance costs, and never reopened to the public. My dad, grandfather, and I, along with Mr. Wickes and others took out all of the diving boards and cement platform in the late 50's. I have been privileged to fish lake Wehi all of my life. What a wonderful part of my life, with many wonderful life long memories. Thank you Wickes family.